A Syllabus of Folk-Songs

Hubert G. Shearin and Josiah Henry Combs

Alpha Editions

This edition published in 2024

ISBN : 9789366388137

Design and Setting By
Alpha Editions
www.alphaedis.com
Email - info@alphaedis.com

As per information held with us this book is in Public Domain.
This book is a reproduction of an important historical work. Alpha Editions uses the best technology to reproduce historical work in the same manner it was first published to preserve its original nature. Any marks or number seen are left intentionally to preserve its true form.

INTRODUCTION

This syllabus, or finding-list, is offered to lovers of folk-literature in the hope that it may not be without interest and value to them for purposes of comparison and identification. It includes 333 items, exclusive of 114 variants, and embraces all popular songs that have so far come to hand as having been "learned by ear instead of by eye," as existing through oral transmission—song-ballads, love-songs, number-songs, dance-songs, play-songs, child-songs, counting-out rimes, lullabies, jigs, nonsense rimes, ditties, etc.

There is every reason to believe that many more such await the collector; in fact, their number is constantly being increased even today by the creation of new ones, by adaptation of the old, and even by the absorption and consequent metamorphosis, of literary, quasi-literary, or pseudo-literary types into the current of oral tradition.

This collection, then, is by no means complete: means have not been available for a systematic and scientific search for these folk-songs, which have been gathered very casually during the past five years through occasional travel, acquaintanceship, and correspondence in only the twenty-one following counties: Fayette, Madison, Rowan, Elliott, Carter, Boyd, Lawrence, Morgan, Johnson, Pike, Knott, Breathitt, Clay, Laurel, Rockcastle, Garrard, Boyle, Anderson, Shelby, Henry, and Owen—all lying in Central and Eastern Kentucky.

All of the material listed has thus been collected in this State, though a variant of The Jew's Daughter, page 8, has come by chance from Michigan, and another of The Pretty Mohee, page 12, was sent from Georgia. The Cumberland Mountain region, in the eastern part of the State, has naturally furnished the larger half of the material, because of local conditions favorable to the propagation of folk-song. However, sections of Kentucky lying farther to the westward are almost equally prolific. The wide extension of the same ballad throughout the State argues convincingly for the unity of the Kentucky stock—a fact which may be confirmed in more ways than one.

The arrangement is as follows: The material in hand is loosely grouped in eighteen sections, according to origin, chronology, content, or form. Though logically at fault, because of the cross-division thus inevitably entailed, this plan has seemed to be the best. No real confusion will result to the user in consequence. In fact, no matter what system be adopted, certain songs will belong equally well to two or more different categories.

Under each of these eighteen main divisions the treatment of the individual song-ballad is in general as follows: First, stands the title, with variant titles in parentheses. Should this be unknown, a caption coined by the editors is placed in brackets. Secondly, a Roman numeral immediately follows the above to denote the number of versions, if variants have been found. Thirdly, the prosodical character of the song is roughly indicated by a combination of letters and numerals. Each letter indicates a line; the variation in the letters indicates, in the usual fashion, the rime-scheme of the stanza. Each numeral indicates the number of stresses in the line (or lines) denoted by the letter (or letters) immediately succeeding it. When a chorus, burden, or refrain is present, the metrical scheme of this stands immediately after an "and," as, for example, in The Blue and the Gray, page 14. In the case of the refrain, the letters used are independent of those immediately preceding the "and," and denoting the rime-scheme of the stanza proper. Fourthly, an Arabic numeral follows to indicate the number of stanzas in the song, exclusive of the refrain, should one be present. If the number of stanzas in a ballad is indeterminable, because its form is fragmentary, or because its variant versions differ in length, this fact is indicated by an appended ca (*circa*). Sixth, and last, is a synopsis, or other attempt to give briefly such data as may serve to complete the identification.

Illustration of the third item above may be helpful. Thus in Pretty Polly, on page 7, 4aabb indicates a quatrain riming in couplets, with four stresses in each line. In Jackaro, page 9, 3abcb indicates a quatrain riming alternately, with three stressed syllables in each line. In The King's Daughter, page 7, 4a3b4c3b indicates a quatrain, with only the second and fourth lines riming and with four stresses in the first and third lines and three stresses in the second and fourth. In Johnnie Came from Sea, page 14, 6aa denotes a rimed couplet, with six stresses in each line.

It has, naturally, been difficult at times to decide whether certain stanzas should be counted as couplets, or as quatrains half as long. In such cases, the air, or tune, and other data, often rather subtle, have been employed in making decisions. The quatrain form has in uncertain instances been given the benefit of the doubt. Even thus, certain minor inconsistencies will perhaps be noted. It is hardly necessary to add that assonance freely occurs in the place of rime, and as such it is considered throughout.

All attempt to indicate the prevailing metrical unit, or foot, within the line has been frankly given over. Iambs, dactyls, and their ilk receive scant courtesy from the composer of folk-song, who without qualm or quaver will stretch one syllable, or even an utter silence (caesura), into the time of a complete bar; while in the next breath he will with equal equanimity huddle a dozen syllables into the same period. Consequently, this item, even if it could be indicated, would have scant descriptive value.

It is a pleasant duty to acknowledge gratefully the assistance of those who have transmitted to our hands many of the songs: Mesdames J. W. Combs, W. T. Phillips, Jennie L. Combs, Richard Smith, Martha Smith, Ruth Hackney, W. F. Hays, Ollie Huff, Robin Cornett, Lucy Banks, Sarah Burton, Kittie Jordan, and Ruby Martin; Misses Martha Jent, Maud Dean, Virginia Jordan, Jessie Green, Lizzie Cody, Margaret Combs, Barbara Smith, Helena E. Rose, Sarah Burton, Sarah Hillman, Cordia Bramblett, Nannie S. Graham, Myrtle Wheeler, Melissa Holbrook, Rosetta Wheeler, Ruth Hackney, Ora McDavid, Jeannette McDavid; Messrs. Wm. W. Berry, Chas. Hackney, S. B. Wheeler, R. L. Morgan, Enoch Wheeler, Thos. H. Hackney, James Goodman, W. S. Wheeler, Harry M. Morgan, Henry Lester, T. G. Wheeler, C. F. Bishop, and John C. Jones.

Especially helpful as collaborators have been Messrs. Winfred Cox, Emory E. Wheeler, Roud Shaw, A. B. Johnston, C. E. Phillips, and H. Williamson.

Kind words or letters of appreciation and, in some cases, of suggestion, from the following have encouraged the preparation of this syllabus: Professors Alexander S. Mackenzie, of the Kentucky State University; Clarence C. Freeman, of Transylvania University; John A. Lomax, of the University of Texas; Albert H. Tolman, of the University of Chicago; John M. McBride, Jr., of the University of the South; George Lyman Kittredge, of Harvard University; Henry M. Belden, of the University of Missouri; and Katherine Jackson, formerly of Bryn Mawr College, who has most generously given the use of her manuscript collection. None of the shortcomings of this brochure, however, can be imputed to them in the slightest degree.

I.

The songs in this group are the survivors of English and Scottish originals, found for the most part in the Child collection. Certain of those given in sections II to XVIII below could doubtless, with due effort, be identified in like manner.

THE KING'S DAUGHTER (SIX PRETTY FAIR MAIDS, PRETTY POLLY), iv, 4a3b4c3b, 9ca: Variants of Lady Isabel and the Elf Knight, Child, No. 4. By a stratagem she drowns the lover just as he is about to drown her.

PRETTY POLLY, iv, 4aabb, 9ca: Parallel in general plot to the above, save that she is led by the lover to an open grave and there slain. (Cf. 5, page 28.)

FAIR ELLENDER, 4a3b4c3b, 10: A variant of the Earl Brand cycle, Child, No. 7.

LORD OF OLD COUNTRY, 4aa, with refrain as below, 10ca: A variant of The Two Sisters, Child, No. 10.

The miller was hung upon Fish-gate, Bosodown,The miller was hung upon Fish-gate,(These sons were sent to me)The miller was hung upon Fish-gateFor drowning of my sister Kate!I'll be true, true to my true-love,If my love'll be true to me.

THE ROPE AND THE GALLOWS (LORD RANDAL), 4aa, 12ca: A variant of Lord Randal, Child, No. 12.

EDWARD, 4a3b4c3b, 10: A variant of the Old World ballad of the same name, Child, No. 13.

THE GREENWOOD SIDE (THREE LITTLE BABES), ii, 4a3b4c3b, 9: Variants of The Cruel Mother, Child, No. 20.

LITTLE WILLIE, 4a3b4c3b, 5: A variant of The Two Brothers, Child, No. 49.

LORD BATEMAN (THE TURKISH LADY), ii, 4abcb, 17ca: Variants of Young Beichan, Child, No. 53.

LOVING HENRY (SWEET WILLIAM AND FAIR ELLENDER), iii, 4a3b4c3b, 11ca: Variants of Young Hunting, Child, No. 68.

LORD THOMAS AND FAIR ELLENDER, iii, 4a3b4c3b, 17ca: Variants of Lord Thomas and Fair Elinor, Child, No. 73.

FAIR MARGARET AND SWEET WILLIAM, iv, 4a3b4c3b, 15ca: Variants of the Old World ballad of the same name, Child, No. 74. (Published by Combs in Jour. Am. Folklore, 23.381.)

LORD LOVELY, 4a3b4c3b, 9: A variant of Lord Lovel, Child, No. 75.

COLD WINTER'S NIGHT (BOSOM FRIEND, LOVER'S FAREWELL), vii, 4a3b4c3b, 9ca: Variants of The Lass of Loch Royal, Child, No. 76. (Published by Shearin, Mod. Lang. Review, Oct., 1911, p. 514.)

LORD VANNER'S (DANIEL'S) WIFE, ii, 4a3b4c3b, 17ca: Variants of Little Musgrave and Lady Barnard, Child, No. 81.

BARBARA ALLEN, vi, 4a3b4c3b, 11ca: Variants of Barbara Allen's Cruelty, Child, No. 84.

THE BAILIFF'S DAUGHTER OF ISLINGTON, 4a3b4c3b, 12: A variant of the Old World ballad of the same name, Child, No. 105.

THE JEW'S DAUGHTER, ii, 4a3b4c3b, 12ca: Variants of Sir Hugh, Child, No. 155. One of the Kentucky versions makes the murdered boy's mother go seeking him switch in hand, to punish him for not returning home before nightfall. (Communicated by Dr. Katherine Jackson.)

THE HOUSE CARPENTER, iii, 4a3b4c3b, 13ca: Variants of The Demon Lover, Child, No. 243.

DANDOO: A fragmentary variant of The Wife Wrapt in Wether's Skin, Child, No. 277, as follows:

He put the sheepskin to his wife's back, Dandoo;He put the sheepskin to his wife's back,Clima cli clash to ma clingo,He put the sheepskin to his wife's back,And he made the old switch go whickity-whack, Then rarum scarum skimble arumSkitty-wink skatty-winkClima cli clash to ma clingo.

THE GREEN WILLOW TREE, metre as below, 11: A variant of The Golden Vanitee, Child, No. 286.

There was a ship sailed for the North Amerikee,From down in the lonesome Lowlands low—There was a ship sailed for the North Amerikee,And she went by the name of the Green Willow Tree,And she sailed from the Lowlands low.

THE DRIVER BOY (YOUNG EDWIN), 4a3b4c3b, 12; The above adapted to a recital of Emily's love for the mail-driver boy and of his untimely murder.

PRETTY PEGGY O, metre as below, 6: A fine lilting lyric of the Captain's love for his lass; his farewell; and his death. It begins:

As we marched down to Fernario, As we marched down to Fernario, Our captain fell in love with a lady like a dove, And they called her by name Pretty Peggy, O.

(Cf. Child, No. 299, Trooper and Maid. Published by Shearin, Sewanee Review, July, 1911, p. 326.)

LADY GAY, 4a3b4c3b, 9: An English woman sends her three children to America. They die on board ship, their shades return to the mother at Christmas and warn her against pride. (Cf. Child, No. 79, The Wife of Usher's Well, and a close variant from North Carolina in Kittredge's Edition, p. 170.)

JACKARO, iv, 3abcb, 17ca: The daughter of a London silk merchant loves Jack, the sailor-boy, against her father's will. Disguised as a man, she follows him to "the wars of Germany," finds him wounded on the battlefield, and nurses him back to health; then they are married. (Cf. Child, 1857 ed., iv, p. 328. The Merchant's Daughter of Bristow, 4abab, 65: Maudlin disguised as a seaman follows her lover to Padua; they are married, and return to England.)

THE FAN, ii, 4abcb, 12: A sea-captain and a lieutenant woo a lady. To test their love she throws her fan into a den of lions. The sea-captain recovers it and wins her. (Published by Shearin, Mod. Lang. Notes, 26. 113; for British originals see Belden, Sewanee Review, April, 1911, p. 218, and Kittredge, Mod. Lang. Notes, 26. 168.)

THE APPRENTICE BOY, iii, 4abcb, 12ca: Like Keats's Isabella, the daughter of a merchant in a post-town loves her father's apprentice. He is slain by her brothers and his body hidden in a valley. His ghost reveals the murderers, who, striving to flee, are lost at sea. (Identified by Belden with an English version, The Constant Farmer's Son, in The Sewanee Review, April, 1911, p. 222.)

II.

The songs in this group are apparently of British origin. Material has not been at hand to justify an attempt to establish their identity.

THE RICH MARGENT [MERCHANT], 2abcb, 12: Dinah, daughter of a rich London merchant, loves Felix contrary to her father's wishes. Going into the garden she drinks poison. Felix arrives and drains the rest of the potion. Both are buried in one grave.

BENEATH THE ARCH OF LONDON BRIDGE, 4a3b4c3b and 4aaaa, 5ca: Here a man, whose son has recently died, finds a waif. Struck by his resemblance to his own heir, he adopts the orphan boy.

JACK WILSON, ii, 4a3b4c3b, 9: The confession of Jack Wilson, a Thames boatman, awaiting execution in Newgate prison for robbery done in Katherine Street, and his denunciation of the "false deluding girl" for whose sake he had done the wrong.

THE OLD WOMAN OF LONDON, 3abcb, 6: She causes her husband to suck two magic marrowbones, which blind him; then leading him to the river, she essays to push him in to drown. But he steps aside, and she dies in his stead. The refrain is:

Sing tidri-i-odre-erdri-um, Sing fol-de-ri-o-day!

THE GOLDEN GLOVE, ii, 4aabb, 9: A mariner's daughter, about to be married to a young squire of London, feigns illness, goes a-hunting on the estate of her favored lover, a farmer, intentionally drops her glove, and vows she will marry only the man who can return it. Of course, the farmer is the lucky finder.

SHEARFIELD, 3abcb, 15: An apprentice in Sheffield recites his running away to London, where he enters the service of an Irish Lady, who falls in love with him. He, however, cares only for Polly Girl, her maid. His jealous mistress, by a stratagem, causes him to be hanged for theft.

FAIR NOTAMON [NOTTINGHAM] TOWN, 4aabb, 7: An absurd recital, full of obvious contradictions, of a countryman's visit to the city, where he sees the royal progress:

I called for a quart to drive gladness awayTo stifle the dust—it had rained the whole day.

LOVELY CAROLINE OF OLD EDINBORO (EDDINGSBURG TOWN), ii, 3abcb, 9: She weds young Henry, "a Highland man," and goes with him to London. Deserted by him, she wanders forlorn to a sea-cliff and plunges in, to drown.

WHO'LL BE KING BUT CHARLIE?, metre as below, 3: A rally-song upon the landing of Charles Stuart, The Young Pretender, at Mordart, in Inverness-shire, July, 1745, beginning:

There's news from Mordart came yestreen,Will soon yastremony (sic) ferly,For ships o'er all have just come inAnd landed royal Charlie.

(Published by Shearin, Sewanee Review, July, 1911, p. 323.)

CUBECK'S [CUPID'S] GARDEN, 3abcb, 16: The poet overhears a lady and her father's apprentice a-courting in "Cubeck's Garden." The angry parent banishes the lad, who goes to sea, is promoted, draws forty thousand pounds in a lottery, returns and marries his fair love.

WILLIAM HALL, ii, 4abcb, 11ca: He is a young farmer of "Domesse-town" and loves a "gay young lady" of "Pershelvy-town" against her parents' wishes. Banished by them to sea, he returns, finds by a ruse that the lady is yet faithful, and marries her.

ROSANNA, 4aabb, 6ca (fragmentary): Silimentary, the lover, bids Rosanna farewell, and is later lost at sea; at the news she stabs herself with a silver dagger.

MARY OF THE WILD MOOR, 3ab4c3b, 8: She, with her babe, returns one winter night to her father's door to seek forgiveness and protection, is rebuffed by him, and perishes in the snow.

BETSY BROWN, 4aabb, 8: John loves Betsy, the waiting-maid; his old mother objects and packs her off across the sea. He dies of grief.

THE ROMISH LADY, 6aabb (or 3abcb), 12 (or 24): "Brought up in popery," she obtains a Bible and turns Protestant, is tried before the Pope, is condemned, bids farewell to mother, father, and tormentors, and is burned at the stake.

III.

The songs of this group are connected more or less closely with American colonial times. For most of them it is fair to infer a British origin.

[TO AMERICA], ii, 4aabb, 8ca: An [English] sailor, bound for America to serve his King, is forgotten by his sweetheart. Returning to her father's hall, he finds her married, and vows to return to Charlestown, where cannonballs are flying.

THE SILK MERCHANT'S DAUGHTER, 2aa, 17: A London lad and his sweetheart set sail for America. The ship springs a leak, the passengers drift in a long-boat. Lot falls to the girl to be slain, her lover takes her place. A passing ship carries them back to London, and they are married.

THE PRETTY MOHEE (MAUMEE), iii, 4aabb, 7: An Indian maid falls in love with a young adventurer and wooes him. He tells her he must return to his love across the sea. This he does, but dissatisfied returns to the "pretty Mohee."

SWEET JANE. 4a3b4c3b, 12: Her lover sails for America "to dig the golden ore," "loads up" his trunk with it, and after many trials reaches home, across the main, and reclaims his bride.

IV.

The songs of this group find their common bond in their reference to Ireland, where some of them undoubtedly had their origin.

IRISH MOLLY O, 6aabb and 6aabb(?), 7: A Scotch laddie, MacDonald, falls in love with "Irish Molly." Scorned by her parents, he wanders about, signifying his intention to die for her, and suggests an appropriate inscription for his tombstone. (See an Old World variant in Brooke and Rolleston's Treasury of Irish Poetry, p. 15, Macmillan, 1905.)

WILLIAM RILEY, 6aabb, 7: Eloping with Polly Ann, he is brought back to trial by her irate father, is defended by an aged lawyer, is transported, and departs wearing the maiden's ring. (See an Old World variant in the volume just named, p. 6.)

ROVING IRISH BOY, 4a3b4c3b, 12: He lands in Philadelphia and "makes a hit" with the ladies. Then he visits "other parts"—among the Dutch of Bucks County, he meets an inn-keeper's daughter, and leaves off rambling.

THE WAXFORD GIRL, 4a3b4c3b, 6: A youth murders his sweetheart and throws her into a stream. He tells his mother, who sees the blood on his clothes, that his nose has been bleeding. He is haunted by the ghost of the dead girl. (Cf. Lizzie Wan, Child, No. 51, and Miller-boy, page 28.)

PATTY ON THE CANAL, 3abcb and 3abcb, 9: Pat lands in "Sweet Philadelphy" and soon "makes himself handy" on the canal, likewise among the girls, whose mothers become anxious. He is a "Jackson man up to the handle."

MOLLY, 6aabb, 4: An Irish lad comes to America, courts Molly, but against her parents' will. He goes to serve a foreign king for seven years, returns, and finds that Molly has died of grief.

JOHNNIE CAME FROM SEA, 6aa, 10: Irish Johnnie escapes a shipwreck and lands in America. Thinking him penniless, a landlord refuses him his daughter's hand. Johnnie "draws out handfuls of gold" and departs, to drink "good brandy."

IRISH GIRL, a fragment, as follows:

So costly were the robes of silkThe Irish girl did wear—Her hair was as black as a raven,Her eyes were black as a crow,Her cheeks were red as rosesThat in the garden grow.

V.

The songs of this group are based upon incidents or events of the Civil War.

BOUNTY JUMPERS, 3abcb, 9: Sam Downey, a soldier, "jumps his bounty," and is apprehended in Baltimore. Refusing to return the money, he is shot by the military authorities.

HIRAM HUBBERT, 3abcb, 9: Hiram Hubbert is taken by the Rebels in the guerrilla warfare in the Cumberland Mountains, tried, tied to a tree and shot. He leaves a last letter of farewell to his family.

THE GUERRILLA MAN, 3a3b4c3b, 5: A Southern soldier goes to Shelby County, Ky., and falls in love with a "Rebel girl," who loves him in spite of the opposition of her mother, and determines to follow him.

MURFREESBORO, 4a3b4c3b, 7: A Union soldier lies dying on the battlefield. He sends to his mother and sweetheart a message recounting his bravery.

BATTLE OF GETTYSBURG (THE TWO SOLDIERS), ii, 4a3b4c3b, 13: Two comrades promise each other to bear messages, in the event of death to either of them on the field—one to a sweetheart, the other to a mother.

THE BLUE AND THE GRAY, 4a3b4c3b4d3e4f4e and 4a3b4c3b3e4f3e, 2: A mother has lost two sons in gray, at Appomattox and at Chickamauga. Her third has just died in blue at Santiago.

ZOLLICOFFER: A fragment as follows:

Old Zollicoffer's dead, and the last word he saidWas, "I'm going back South; they're a-gaining."If he wants to save his soul, he had better keep his hole,Or we'll land him in the happy land of Canaan.

I'M GOING TO JOIN THE ARMY, 3abcb, 12: A volunteer's farewell to his sweetheart as he leaves for Pensacola, her fears, and his promise to return.

[COME ALL, YE SOUTHERN SOLDIERS], 3abcb, 8: A volunteer, aged sixteen, from Eastern Tennessee, describes the march into Virginia and his feelings at his first sight of the "Yankees."

VI.

The songs of this group relate to the days of pioneer migration Westward. The one exception is The Sailor's Request, placed here in order to bring it into proximity with its later variant, The Dying Cowboy.

ARKANSAS TRAVELLER (SANTFORD BARNES) ii, 4a3b4c3b, 14ca: A laborer's humorous recital of his hard experiences in Arkansas. He leaves the state, vowing that if he sees it again it will be "through a telescope from hell to Arkansaw."

STARVING TO DEATH ON A GOVERNMENT CLAIM, 4aa and 4aabb, 20: "Ernest Smith" recites humorously his hard experiences as claim-holder in Beaver County, Oklahoma. He resolves to go to Kansas, marry, and "life on corn-dodgers the rest of his life."

THE DYING COWBOY, ii, 4abcb and 4abcb, 6: A cowboy, shot while gambling, laments his career and fate, gives warning to his comrades, sends a farewell to his family and sweetheart, and gives directions for his funeral.

THE LONE PRAIRIE, 4aabb, 10: A dying cowboy requests that he be buried not on the lone prairie, but at home beneath the cotton-wood boughs, near his mother. His comrades ignore his petition. (Cf. The Sailor's Request.)

THE SAILOR'S REQUEST, 4aabb, 9: A dying sailor requests that he be buried not at sea, but at home in the churchyard, near his father. His comrades ignore his petition. (Cf. The Lone Prairie.)

CALIFORNIA JOE, 3abcb, 17: A prospector during the California gold-fever, in 1850, saves a girl of thirteen years from Indians, and gives her over to her uncle, Mat Jack Reynolds. Later, she almost shoots, by accident, her saviour, thinking him a Sioux.

POLLY, MY CHARMER, 4aa, 9: An adventurous youth, on the point of going West, is detained by the charms of "Polly." He wishes he were like Joshua, in order to prolong his moments with his love, by making the sun stand still.

JESSE JAMES, 2aa3b2cc3b and 2aa3b2cc3b, 4: A lyric concerning the robbing of "the Danville train" and "the Northfield raid"; the escape of Jesse and Frank James to the West, and Jesse's death at the hand of "Bob Ford."

HANDSOME FLORA, 3abcbdefe, 6: Her lover, in prison for stabbing his rival, tells his yet constant devotion to the "Lily of the West," the "girl from Mexico."

VII.

The songs of this group are of the "good-night" type, being the meditations or confessions of criminals, while in prison and, usually, under sentence of death.

MACAFEE'S CONFESSION (BETTY STOUT), ii, 4aabb, 17ca: Orphaned at five years of age and reared by his uncle, MacAfee becomes wayward; later he marries, but falls in love with Betty Stout, poisons his wife, and speaks this confession under sentence of death.

BEAUCHAMP'S CONFESSION, 4aabb, 7: Under sentence of death by Judge Davidge, for the murder of Sharpe (see VIII, end), Beauchamp pictures the meeting of himself and his victim in hell.

JACK COMBS'S DEATH SONG, ii, 4abcb and 4abcb, 3: Jack Combs, dying, tells of his murder by an unknown man, and gives directions for his burial rites. (Based upon The Dying Cowboy, page 15.)

TOM SMITH'S DEATH SONG, ii, 3a(*bis*)4b3c and 3a(*bis*) 4b3c, 2: The condemned man, standing on the scaffold, asks his friends not to lament his death, since he is leaving them in peace on earth.

THE RICH AND RAMBLING BOY, iii, 4aabb, 8ca: He marries a wife whose "maintenance" is so great that he is compelled to "rob on the broad highway." He is sent to Frankfort [Ky.] prison, but in this song he pictures his pardon and return home.

[IN ROWAN COUNTY JAIL], 3abcb, 6: While here awaiting trial for robbery, the prisoner is visited by his sweetheart Lula, with "ten dollars in each hand," to "go on his bail."

LAST NIGHT AS I LAY SLEEPING, 3abcb, 6: A prisoner in the Knoxville [Tenn.] jail dreams of his home and sweetheart, but is rudely awakened by the turnkey to hear his death-sentence passed.

EDWARD HAWKINS, 4abcb, 9ca: Under sentence of death for murder, he warns his comrades by his example, welcomes death bravely, and invites them to see his execution twenty-eight days hence.

ROWDY BOYS, metre as below, 5: A "rowdy" youth scorns his mother's warning, serves a term in the Frankfort State Prison for homicide, and comes back home still a "rowdy." The first stanza is:

I heard my mother talking; I took it all for fun.She said I would ride the Frankfort train, before I was twenty-one.

VIII.

The songs of this group are epic; rather than lyric as are those in VII, above. They are recitals of local tragedies—murders, assassinations, feudal battles, and disasters.

THE CAUSE AND KILLING OF JESSE ADAMS, ii, 3abcb, 25: A detailed recital of a domestic tragedy on the Brushy Fork of Blaine: Adams, overhearing his wife and her paramour, shoots her and attempts suicide.

FLOYD FRAZIER, 3abcb, 16: A recital of Frazier's murder of Ellen Flannery: he hides her body under a pile of stones; later, is arrested, makes confession, and is placed in Pineville, Ky., jail to await execution.

TALT HALL, ii, 3abcb, 8: A recital of Hall's murder of Frank Salyers, his arrest in Tennessee, his confinement in the Gladeville, Va., jail, and his execution in Richmond, Va.

WILLIAM BAKER, 3abcb, 12: A recital of Baker's murder of one Prewitt in Clay County, Ky.: he hides the body in the woods and tells Prewitt's wife that her husband had deserted her.

POOR GOENS, 4aabb, 5: A recital of the betrayal and murder of Goens for the purpose of robbery, on Black-spur Mountain.

THE ROWAN COUNTY TRAGEDY, ii, 3abcb, 26: A detailed account of a feudal battle in Morehead, Ky., on election day, and of the succeeding events connected with the arrest of the participants.

JOHN T. PARKER, 4aabb, 12: An account of the drowning of Parker in the Kentucky River one winter night, as, with three companions, he essays to cross, but their boat is capsized in the wash from the steamboat Blue Wings.

[JEEMS BRAGGS], 4a3b4c3b, 8: A protest against the Governor's pardon of Braggs, upon the eve of his execution, for the murder of one Prewitt.

THE ASSASSINATION OF J. B. MARCUM, 3aa6b3cc6b and 3aa6b3cc6b, 13: A detailed recital of the shooting of Marcum as he stood in the court-house door at Jackson, Ky., with animadversions upon the identity of his slayers and an account of their various trials.

THE IRISH PEDDLER, 4a3b4c3b, 7: An account of the murder of an old peddler and his wife, shot from ambush one June morning for the purpose of rifling their wagon.

JOHN HARDY, iii, 4a3b4c3b, 6: An account of Hardy's shooting a man in a poker game, of his arrest, trial, conviction, conversion and baptism, and of his execution and burial on the Tug River.

JEREBOAM BEAUCHAMP, 3abcb, 33: A recital of the murder of Beauchamp done upon Solomon P. Sharpe, Attorney-General of Kentucky, at Frankfort in the winter of 1824. (Cf. William Gilmore Simms' novel of the same name, and see VII, 2.)

IX.

The songs of this group relate to various occupational pursuits. Of course, many of those listed elsewhere could be placed here also.

THE MOONSHINER, 4aa, 3: "For seventeen years I've made moonshine whiskey for one dollar per gallon, at my still in a dark hollow. I wish all would attend to their business and leave me to mine. God bless the moonshiner!"

WALKING-BOSS, metre as below, 3: A teamster's song in couplets, with refrain, beginning:

Get up in the morning 'way before day,Feed old Beck some corn and hay.Get up in the morning soon, soon;Get up in the morning soon.

THE STEEL-DRIVER, ii, 4a3b4c3b, 11: John Henry, proud of his skill with sledge and hand-drill, competes with a modern steam-drill in Tunnel No. Nine, on the Chesapeake & Ohio Railroad. Defeated, he dies, asking to be buried with his tools at his breast.

ROSIN THE BOW, 3abcb, 4: A lyric of an old fiddler buoyant even in the face of approaching death: he asks for wine and women at his funeral rites.

ROSIN THE BOW: a fragment as follows:

I'll tune up my fiddle, I'll rosin my bow,And make myself welcome wherever I go.

THE OLD SHOEMAKER, 4a3b4c3b and 4a3b4c3b, 4: Lately become a freeman, with five pounds laid up, and half a side of leather, he sings of Kate, the woman to make his content complete.

THE FARMER'S BOY, ii, 4a3b4c3b, 9: An orphan lad, he obtains employment from the farmer, later to marry his daughter and inherit thus the farm.

OLD GRAY, 6aabb, 5: Song of a teamster, who, lured by the still-house, hauls four loads of coal per day, instead of six; becoming drunk, he rides Old Gray off to a country frolic one night, whither his father follows him, and brings him back to his duty in the morning.

THE WAGGONER'S LAD, ii, 2abcb (or 4aa), 15: A complaint, arranged as a *debat*, of a lorn and loving lass against the teamster lad, as he departs from her.

OLD NUMBER FOUR (THE F. F. V., STOCKYARD GATE), ii, 6aabb, 10ca: George Allen, engineer, stays at the throttle as train Number Four on the Chesapeake & Ohio Railroad plunges into a fallen boulder near Hinton, W. Va., and bids his fireman jump to safety, while he himself dies a hero's death.

[RAILROAD BOY], 4a3b4c3b and 4a3b4c3b, 5: A maiden's song in scorn of all men save the railroad conductor, with his striped shirt, handsome face, and diamond ring.

THE OLD MILLER, 4aabb, 7: Dying, he questions his sons in order to choose one of them as his successor in the mill. Dick will take a peck as toll from each bushel; Ralph will take half; Paul will take all. But his wife assumes direction at his death.

LYNCHBURG TOWN, 4a3b4c3b, 3: A teamster's song as he takes his tobacco to the Lynchburg (Va.) market.

X.

The songs of this group are of partisan or sectional character.

KAINTUCKY BOYS, 4abab and 4ab, 5. A *debat* between a Virginia lad and the Kentucky maiden whom he comes to woo. She scorns lands and money, and lauds the superior manliness of the Kentucky lads.

BUCKSKIN BOYS, 4abab 9: The above adapted to the praises of the "boys" of Owsley County (Ky.).

GOEBEL AND TAYLOR, 4a3b4c3d, 3: Composed soon after the assassination of Wm. Goebel, the Democratic contestant for the Governorship of Kentucky in 1900: He is lauded, while Taylor, his opponent, is condemned as a demagogue and conspirator, who "ought to be in purgatory or some other unhealthy spot."

JAMES A. GARFIELD: A fragment, as follows:

Mr. James A. Garfield is dead,Oh, Mr. James A. Garfield is dead.I will weep like a willow,And I'll mourn like a dove;Mr. James A. Garfield is dead.

XI.

Here are grouped songs whose main theme is love, subdivided as below. Many are hardly "popular" in the strict sense: though current among the folk, they differ from the true folk-song, or "song-ballet." On the other hand, many bear a striking resemblance to certain of those listed in I and II, above.

1. SONGS OF CONSTANT LOVE.

AVONIA (RED RIVER VALLEY), ii, 4a3b4c3b and 4a3b4c3b, 4: A constant lover's song of farewell to Helen, as she leaves the vale of Avonia.

BARNEY AND KATE, 4abab, 6: Barney, maudlin with drink, comes one winter's night to Kate's window and implores her to admit him. She sends him packing. He goes away whistling, rejoicing in her chastity.

KITTY WELLS, 4ababcdcd and 3abab, 3. Her lover's Lament upon her death. The refrain is:

While the birds they were singing in the morning,And the ivy and the myrtle were in bloom,The sun on the hill-top was dawning,It was then we laid her in the tomb.

NORA O'NEIL, 4a3b4a3b, 5: Her lover's invitation to Nora to meet him "at the foot of the lane" when the nightingale sings in the dusk.

SWEET BIRDS, ii, 4a3b4a3b and 5aa, 6: A maiden's song of longing for her absent lover: she asks the birds to bear her message of devotion to him and to bring him back secure in his affection for her.

[CONSTANT JOHNNY], 4aa, 14: A maiden sings her devotion to her absent sailor lover. He returns and they are married.

LORLA, 4aabb, 2: A lover's elegy over the grave of Lorla beneath the elm, as he recalls the golden willow under which they once sat on violet banks.

LONESOME DOVE, 4a3b4c3b, 5: A constant husband sings his resolve to return like a lonesome dove to his wife and children in "Californy."

LONESOME DOVE, 4aabb, 8: The singing of a dove bereft of its mate reminds a constant husband of his Mary, recently dead of consumption.

PRETTY SARO, iii, 4aabb and 4aabb, 6ca: Her absent lover sings of his devotion, wishing he were a priest and knew how to write to her, or a dove to fly to her.

COME, ALL YE JOLLY BOATSMAN BOYS, 7aabb, 5: A ribald song of a sailor to his amorata by night, and the birth of the child nine months later.

A PACKAGE OF OLD LETTERS, ii, 8aa, 11: A dying maiden bids her sister bring them from their rosewood casket to read them to her again, and asks that at her death they be buried with her.

JACK AND MAMIE, 6aabb and 4aaa3a, 4: Jack plunges into the water to recover the hat of his girl sweetheart, Mamie. Jack, the man, leaves her for a long voyage, and his ship never returned.

SWEET SUMMER EVENING, 4abcb, 7: The poet one summer evening overhears a mother chide her daughter for her devotion to her roving sailor lover, who soon appears and bids her an affectionate farewell.

WAIT FOR THE WAGON, 3abcbdefe and 4a(*ter*), 4: A lover's call to Phyllis to jump into the wagon with him a-Sunday morning; he tells her of the cabin he has built for her, and wooes her to marry him.

LOVELY NANCY, 4abcb, 5: A dialogue, in quatrains, between Nancy and her lover, whom she wishes to accompany on his voyage to the West Indies.

NANCY TILL, 4aabb and 4aabb, 4: A serenade by her lover "down in the canebrakes close by the mill," urging her to be ready to go with him "a-sailing on the Ohio."

[EPHRIAM AND LUCY], 4a3b4c3b and 4a3b4c3b, 4: The night before their wedding-day, amid night-hawks, owls, and whippoorwills, "we danced by the light of the moon."

2. SONGS OF LOVE INCONSTANT.

[SHE WAS HAPPY TILL SHE MET YOU], 4aa5b4cc5b4dd5e4ff5e and 4ababcc5b, 2: A husband forsakes his wife; later, becoming repentant, he returns to seek her at the house of her mother, who forbids him access to her.

[BEDROOM WINDOW], 4abcb, 5: The lover by night calls his sweetheart to awake. She warns him away, saying that her father is armed to repulse his presence. He vows to have her for his own. A suggestion of his sinister motive closes the song.

I'LL HANG MY HARP ON A WILLOW TREE, ii, 4a3b4a3b4c3d4c3d, 3: A lover voices his resolve to forsake the charms of his fickle mistress to court a warrior's fate at the Saracen's hand on the field of Palestine.

THERE WAS A RICH OLD FARMER, ii, 3abcb, 9ca: The singer recites his farewell to father and sweetheart to seek his fortune, and his faith in her—until a letter arrives telling of her marriage to another man.

JACK AND JOE, 4a3b4b3c and 4a3b4b3c, 3ca: Both are sailors, away from home. Jack, returning first, is commissioned by Joe to kiss his sweetheart Nellie for him. When Joe returns, like Miles Standish, he finds that Jack and she are married.

ALL ON THE BANKS OF CLAUDA, 3abcb, 10: By this stream the poet overhears a maiden's complaint against her fickle Johnny. Like Oenone, she prays the mountain to hear her, and implores Cupid to fire his heart anew.

THE AUXVILLE LOVE, 4aabb, 6: A merchant's daughter, "in Auxville town or Delaware," love-lorn, gathers flowers, Ophelia-like, and dies under a green pine on the mountain.

CUCKOO, ii, 4aabb, 5ca: A love-lorn maiden's warning to her sex not to be deceived, as she, by false men in springtime when the cuckoo calls.

WE HAVE MET AND WE HAVE PARTED, ii, 4abcb and 4abcb, 5ca: A maiden's scornful farewell to her fickle lover, as she returns him the presents and letters he has sent her.

IF I HAD MINDED MAMMA, 3abcb and 3abcb, 6: A maiden's regret that she has been deluded by a faithless lover:

He is like the blue-birds everThat flies from tree to tree;And when he sees another girlHe never thinks of me.

I USED TO LOVE, 4abcb and 4abcb, 4: A maiden voices her complaint against the "dark-eyed girl," her successful rival, and her wish for "coffin, shroud, and grave," to end her woe.

THE BUTCHER'S BOY, iii, 4aabb, 8ca: A maiden voices her complaint against the New York butcher's boy, once her childhood playmate and lover, who now has forsaken her for a wealthier girl; then goes upstairs and hangs herself, leaving a note pinned on her breast.

THE PALE AMARANTHUS, 4aabb, 5: A maiden's complaint against her faithless lover, whom she vows to forget.

I HAVE FINISHED HIM A LETTER, 4abcb and 4abcb, 7: A maiden's complaint against her lover, who has forsaken her for Annie Lee.

CAN YOU THEN LOVE ANOTHER?, ii, 3abcbdefe and 3abcb, 3: A lorn maiden's plaint:

Say, must I be forgotten,Cast like a flower aside?Have I from memory faded,Once all your joy and pride?

TO CHEER THE HEART, ii, 3abcbdefe and 3abcbdede, 4: A maiden's complaint against her faithless lover. He is the son of a "rich merchant," she, the daughter of a "laboring man." "But why need I care? For I have another man."

A POOR STRANGE GIRL, 4aabb, 7: The poet one May morning overhears a damsel complaining against her faithless lover, and against her loss of friends and home.

PRETTY POLLY, 4aabb, 5: A lover recites his visit one evening to her home, where he sees his rivals enjoying her company. He retires to a grove, sucks comfort from his whiskey bottle, and wishes that she were drowned, floating on the tide, that he, like a fisherman, might draw her in his net to shore.

HANG DOWN YOUR HEAD AND CRY, 4aabb, 2: A fragment (two quatrains), apparently a complaint of a lover to his faithless sweetheart.

THE DYING GIRL'S MESSAGE, ii, 4abcb, 15: Her death-song to her mother, breathing forgiveness for her faithless lover, and closing with a vision of Christ waiting to receive her.

A second version contains only an elaboration of this last motif.

THE COLD, DARK SCENES OF WINTER, 3abcb, 9: In the winter the lover woos his fair, but is rejected. In the spring, her mind changing, she writes him of her love for him. He replies that meanwhile his heart has changed in turn and that he is already married to another.

LOVING HANNER, 3abcb, 9: The lover sings his devotion to her, but in the face of her coolness and her parents' opposition, vows to go on a long voyage to try to forget her—but in vain.

MY BONNIE LITTLE GIRL, 4a3b4c3b, 4: Courting her too slow, the singer finds his sweetheart has fled with another man.

LOVELY NANCY, ii, 4aabb, 5ca: A bachelor's warning against "courting too slow": Sweet William goes on a voyage; meanwhile Nancy, his sweetheart, writes him of her marriage to another. William dies of grief and Nancy, of remorse.

I'M SCORNED FOR BEING POOR (VAIN GIRL), 3abcb, 8: A lover's farewell to his sweetheart, who has forsaken him to be married to a wealthy stranger from New England.

LITTLE NELLIE, 4a3b4c3b, 8: She forsakes her lover, the singer, to marry wicked, wealthy Mr. Brown, who is a drunkard—and dies of a broken heart.

THE SQUIRE, 2abcb, 10: The wealthy young squire, being rejected in love by pretty Sally, vows to dance on her grave when she dies.

LITTLE SPARROW (A REGRET), ii, 4abcb, 5ca: A complaint of a love-lorn maiden warning her kind against the faithlessness of all men.

THE AWFUL WEDDING, 4abcb, 7: At the marriage feast each guest is asked for a song. The bride's former lover sings his unchanging affection for her. She swoons and spends the night in her mother's bed, where she is found dead the next morning.

THE YOUNG MAN'S LOVE, 2aa, 9: The singer one evening overhears a young man lamenting the faithlessness of his sweetheart, who scorns him for his poverty.

[MAGGIE], 3a3b4c3b and 2abab (approximately), 7: A story of Maggie, the constant wife, who seeks in bar-room and dry-goods store her faithless husband, who has eloped with Lula Fry. Failing to find him, she wanders to the cemetery, and thence to the railroad trestle, where she is killed by train No. Four.

JOE HARDY, 4a3b4c3b, 6: A maiden's explanation to her jilted lover that when she plighted her troth in Bangor, she had not then met Joe Hardy, whom she now adores.

3. SONGS OF LOVE THWARTED.

LOVELY JULIA, iv, 4abcb, 9ca: Crossed in love by her parents, she leaves the city, goes upon a mountain, and plunges a dagger into her breast. Her lover finds her and in like manner dies with her.

JOHNNY DOYLE, 2aa, 14ca: A maiden, who loves Johnny, is forced by her parents to prepare to marry Samuel Moore. Just as the priest enters, her earrings fall to the floor and her stay-laces burst. She is carried home fatally ill. The mother now proposes to send for Johnny Doyle, but it is too late—she is dead.

ANNIE WILLOW, iii, 4a3b4c3b, 8: Her lover dreams of her and goes to her uncle's house to visit her. Upon being told that she is absent, he fights his way in with drawn sword and takes her away with him.

GREENBRIAR SHORE, 4aa, 10: An amorous youth recites his love for Nancy on Greenbriar Shore. Her father chases him away with an "army of a thousand or more." The sad lot of womankind deplored.

4. SONGS OF ABSENT LOVERS REUNITED.

THE SINGLE SOLDIER (THE SAILOR LOVER, JOHN RILEY), v, 4abcb, 8ca: "A pretty fair damsel in a garden" is wooed by a passing soldier (or sailor). She rejects him, saying her lover is absent in the wars. Assured of her faithfulness, he proves his identity by taking their betrothal ring from his pocket.

ANNIE AND WILLIE, 4a3b4c3b, 7: He bids her farewell at the seashore and goes on a long voyage. After three years he returns, and, disguised as a beggar, tests her devotion, draws the "patch from his eye," is recognized, and marries her. (Cf. The Bailiff's Daughter of Islington, page 8, above.)

PRETTY POLLY, 4aabb, 8: Pining for her soldier lover, who is absent in the "town of renown," she goes in the guise of a trooper to seek him, becomes his room-mate for the night, and discloses her identity in the morning.

5. SONGS OF THE MURDEROUS LOVER. (CF. I FOR SIMILAR BALLADS.)

FLORELLA (FLOELLA, FAIR ELLA, JEALOUS LOVER), iv, 3abcb, 11ca: Her lover comes one moonlit night to her cottage window and persuades her to wander with him "through meadows dark and gay." She reluctantly follows, and is murdered by him, forgiving him with her dying breath.

LITTLE OMY WISE (LITTLE ANNA), iii, 4aa, 13: John Lewis seduces her with promises, lures her to Adam's Spring, murders her, and throws her body into the stream. She is "missen," the body is found, the murderer views it and confesses the crime.

MILLER-BOY, ii, 4a3b4c3b, 12ca: Johnny, the miller's apprentice, falls in love with a Knoxville girl. One night the pair go walking; he murders her with a fence-stake, explains the stains on his clothes as due to nose-bleed, but is convicted. (Cf. Lizzie Wan, Child, No. 51, and Waxford Girl, page 13.)

POLLY VAUGHN, 2abcb (approximately), 4ca: One evening dressed in white she goes walking, takes refuge from a shower under a holly bush, is mistaken for a swan by her lover, Jimmy Randal, and shot.

ROSE COLALEE (COLLEEN?), 4a3b4c3b, 2: She is murdered on the bank of a river, by her lover, who, intoxicated with Burgundy wine, is persuaded by his father's promise of money, to slay her.

NOTE.—*Amid the flotsam and jetsam of popular parlor-songs everywhere current the following have come to hand. They are hardly worth preserving, even by title, save for the fact that in spite of their pseudo-literary tang they are fellow travelers by oral tradition with the true folk-songs and song-ballads.*

The list is: The Old, Old Love is Growing Still; There's a Spark of Love Still Burning; I'll Remember You, Love, in My Prayers; The White Rose; I'll Love Thee Always; Jack and Mary; Willie and Kate; Won't You Ever Come Again?; Fond Affection; Will You Love Me When I'm Old?; Nell and I had Quarrels; Tell Me Why You've Grown so Cold?; I Want to be Somebody's Darling; By the Gate; The Broken Engagement; Say You'll be Mine in a Year; I Cannot be Your Sweetheart; Kiss Me Again; Just Going Down to the Gate; Darling, We have Long been Parted; Our Hands are Clasped; Only Flirting; I Loved You Better than You Knew; Mollie Darling; The Jealous Girl; The Independent Girl; Willie, Come Back; Free Again; The Hawthorn Tree; The Sailor Lad; I'll be All Smiles Tonight; Love, I've been Faithful; Maggie's Secret; I Rather Think I Will; Little Sweetheart; Meet Me in the Moonlight; He's Got Money, Too; After the Ball; Sweet Bunch of Daisies; In the Shadow of the Pines; On the Banks of the Wabash; Mary has Gone with a "Coon."

XII.

This group contains two-part songs, arranged dialogue-fashion, like a debat or a tenson. All contain love-themes, as in XI above. In spite of the obvious logical cross-division, it has seemed well to print them as a separate section.

I'LL GIVE TO YOU A PAPER OF PINS, ii, 4aab3b, 13: The lover offers the maiden in alternate quatrains various gifts to induce her to marry him. She replies in alternate quatrains, refusing him. Finally, he offers "the key of his chest." She accepts, but he scorns her mercenary love.

MADAM, I'VE A-COURTING COME, 4a3b4c3b, 7: The lover in the first three quatrains offers his various forms of wealth to induce the lady to marry him. She refuses in the fifth stanza his mercenary love. He makes reply in the sixth and she in the seventh.

TWO LETTERS, ii, 3abcb, 13: The first four quatrains constitute the letter from Charley Brooks to Nelly Adair, asking for the return of his presents to her, since his love for her has grown cold. The last nine are her reply, acquiescing with a sad dignity.

[STONY HILL], 4a3b4c3b, 3: Each quatrain contains, in couplets respectively, question and reply of lover and sweetheart, who is "sixteen next Sunday" and has to "ask her mammy."

STELLA, 4a3b4c3b, 14: A dialogue between Alfred, a volunteer at his country's call, to Stella, his sweetheart.

THE WAGGONER'S LAD: See Section IX.

KAINTUCKY BOYS: See Section X.

BUCKSKIN BOYS: See Section X.

XIII.

This group consists of humorous songs. Certain ones resemble modern songs of the vaudeville, and such they probably were.

GRANDMOTHER'S MUSTARD PLASTER, 4aabb, 7ca: The story of a plaster that drew the buttons from a vest, axles from a wagon, a street car forty miles, jerked a "Chinee's" boot off and pulled his leg at the "opium jint," mashed a "cop's" hat down, drew a wagon over town, stuck on a passenger train, drew it to Washington, where it remained—stuck on politics.

BOY AND BUMBLE-BEE, 4a3b4c3b(?), 5: An urchin puts a bumble-bee in his pistol pocket and goes fishing. He sits down, the bee turns the trick, and "spoils the urchin's disposition."

KATE AND THE CLOTHIER, 4aabb, 8ca: A jilted maiden disguises herself in "an old cowhide with crooked horns," and seizes her clothier-lover in a "lonesome field." Thinking her to be the Devil, he renounces the lawyer's daughter and pledges his troth to Kate.

SEYMORE WILSON, 3a3b4c3b, 8ca: He is a gawky, love-sick youth. He goes a-courting on Potriffle, but finding a rival sitting on the "calico-side" returns to his plowing, weeps, then becomes cheerful in his resolve to wait for another girl.

BILLY BOY, ii, 4a3b4c3b, 7: He replies to a series of questions about his wife: she is "too young to leave her mammy," can "bake a cherry-pie," is "as tall as a pine and as straight as a pumpkin-vine," is "twice six times seven, twice twenty and eleven," and so on.

[THE PREACHER AND THE BEAR], a chant of the 4a3b4c3b type, 7ca: He goes hunting a-Sunday, meets a grizzly bear, climbs a tree, and prays a humorous prayer for help. The limb breaks; he falls, but escapes.

[LOVE IS SUCH A FUNNY THING], 4a3b4c3b4d3e4f3e and 4a3b4c3b, 9: It causes empty pockets, second-hand clothing, collectors, and even brings the "bald-headed end of the broom" into play: a husband's soliloquy.

[THE MARRIED MAN], 4aa, 5: A married man's woes: children on his knees, bad clothing, "seeping" shoes—while the single man suffers none of these things.

DEVILISH MARY, 4a3b4c3b, 5: A hen-pecked husband's lament: he woos and marries the termagant within three days—then follows trouble. She "mashes his mouth with a shovel," bundles up her "duds", and leaves him within three weeks.

I WON'T MARRY AT ALL, 4aab3b and 4aab3b, 3: I won't marry a rich man because he will drink and fall in the ditch; a poor man, for he will go begging; a fat man, for he will do nothing but "nurse" the cat.

POOR OLD MAID, metre as below, 5: She laments her virginity:

Dressed in yaller, pink, and blue—Poor old maid!Dressed in yaller, pink, and blue,I'm just as sweet as the morning dew,And to a husband I'd stick like glue—Poor old maid!

I WISH I WAS SINGLE AGAIN, metre as below, 5: A married man's repentance: his first wife died—

I married me another, O then, O then;I married me another O then;I married me another, the Devil's grandmother,And I wish I was single again.

JOE BOWERS, 3abcb, 10: He leaves his sweetheart, Sally Black, in Pike County, Missouri, and goes to "Rome," California, to make a home for her. Later, he receives a letter from his brother Ike saying that she had married a red-headed butcher and that their baby had red hair.

A POUND OF TOW, 3abcded, 4: A husband warns all bachelors by the example of his own wife, who, though a good spinner before her marriage, has since become a gad-about and a gossip.

XIV.

The songs of this group, in lieu of a better caption, may be called sentimental.

THE BLIND CHILD, iii, 4a3b4c3b, 11ca: She deplores her father's second marriage, kneels to say her evening prayers, and dies. She is buried by the side of her mother.

THE DYING NUN, 4abcb, 12: To Sister Martha, her nurse, Sister Clara tells her youthful waywardness toward her parents and recalls her early love for Douglas, and dies.

THE SHIP THAT NEVER RETURNED, 4a3b4c3b4d3e4f3e, 6: The vanity of human wishes: a feeble lad kissing his mother good-bye as he sets sail to seek health in a foreign climate; a gallant seaman kissing his wife good-bye as he sets sail to seek their fortune across the seas—but the ship of either never returned.

I HAVE NO MOTHER NOW, 3abab, 9: An orphan's lament, with a vision of the mother's grave, etc.

THE ORPHAN GIRL, 4a3b4c3b, 8: Refused shelter at the door of a rich man one wintry night, she dies before it in the snow.

PHANTOM FOOTSTEPS, 4ababcdcd and 4abab, 3: A mother's night-yearning for her dead child.

[THE WAYWARD GIRL], 4aa6b4cc6b4dd6e4ff6e and 4ab2cc4bde2ff4e, 2: One year after leaving her home in wayward love, her father writes her of her mother's death and forgives her, but she refuses to return.

OLD MAN'S TROUBLE, 4aa5b4cc5b and 4aa5b4cc5b, 3: A meditation upon the sadness of old age and a warning to the young against their own days of poverty and senile helplessness.

IN THE BAGGAGE-COACH AHEAD, iii, 4a3b4c3b4d3e4f3e4g3h4i3h and 4aabb, 2: A crying child brings to its sad-eyed father remonstrances from sleepy passengers until they are told that the dead mother is in the baggage-coach ahead.

[SWEET MEMORY OF DEAR MOTHER], 3abcbdefe and 3abcbdefe, 3: A child's loving reminiscence.

LITTLE MAUDIA, 4abcb, 6: A dying girl's farewell to her mother.

OLD CHURCH-YARD, 4abcb, 7: A forlorn orphan's meditation upon her mother's grave.

XV.

The songs of this group, in lieu of a more accurate name, may be called moralities, since they contain a moral incident or reflection.

[THE BLACK SHEEP], 4a3b4c3b4d3e4f3e and 4a3b4c3b4d3e4f3e, 6: Jack and Tom prevail upon their rich and aged father to send away their brother Fred as a "black sheep." Later, just as these two Pharisees are about to send the old man to the poorhouse, Fred reappears and saves him from this disgrace.

[NOTHING TO BE MADE BY ROVING], 3abcb, 2: Dissipation brings discontent at last.

TWO DRUMMERS, 6aabbccdd and 6aabb, 2: In a "grand hotel" they speak slightingly to a pretty waitress. She rebukes them, making appeal to their regard for their mothers. They apologize to her and one of them marries her.

THE DRUNKARD'S DREAM, ii, 4a3b4c3b, 9: A vision of his dead wife and children turns him from strong drink forever after.

FATHER, DEAR FATHER, COME HOME WITH ME NOW, 4a3b4c3b4d3e4f3e and 3a3b4c3b, 3: The little daughter begs her father to come home from the grog-shop before her little brother dies. The clock tolls twelve, one, two, three—and when finally she leads him home, the boy is dead.

A DRIFTER RESCUED, 4abcb, 10: The turbulent journey of a ship-wrecked soul: near the brink of destruction the reckless man finds a redeemer in the Savior.

THE WANDERING BOY, 4aabb and 4abcc, 4: A mother's wail for her wayward son: she points out the vacant chair, cradle, and shoes of his innocent babyhood.

XVI.

This group contains sequence-songs, or number-songs, like the popular German Zaehllieder, though not all are necessarily sung, but rather are spoken. The first one below would seem to be akin to the various cabala of the German Pietists of Pennsylvania.

[TWELVE APOSTLES], as follows:

Twelve, twelve apostles,Eleven, eleven, I went to heaven,Ten, ten, commandments,Nine bright lights a-shining,Eight Gabel [Gabriel?] angels,Seven stars a-hanging high,Six, six go acymord,Five all alone abroard,Four scorn in Wackford,Three of them are drivers,Two of them are little lost babes,Oh, my dear Savior,One, one is left alone,One to be left alone.

CLUB-FIST: A series of questions and answers concerning the fire, water, ox, butcher, rope, rat, cat, etc.—each of which terms is destructive of the preceding one. (Spoken.)

JOHN BROWN'S LITTLE INDIANS: An enumeration of his "Indians" from unity upward, and thence back to unity again.

THE UNLUCKY YOUNG MAN, ii, 4aa and 4aaa3b, 13ca: He exchanges oxen for a cow, the cow for a calf, the calf for a dog, the dog for a cat, the cat for a rat, the rat for a mouse, which "took fire to her tail and burned down the house."

OLD SAM SUCK-EGG, ii, 2aa, 10: He swaps his wife for a duck-egg, and this for other commodities in turn, which rime with each preceding line, until he has lost all. (Spoken.)

[I BOUGHT ME A HORSE], 4aa and cumulative refrain of animal cries: In each couplet a new purchase of some common animal or fowl is made, while each succeeding refrain gathers up cumulative-fashion the cries made by each succeeding addition to the collection.

ONE, TWO, COME BUCKLE MY SHOE, 2aa, 10: A sequence of riming half-lines, each containing a digit up to twenty. (Spoken.)

XVII.

This group contains songs peculiar to the folk-dances, "frolickings," and movement-games of Kentucky.

CHARLIE, ii, 4a3b4c3b, an endless improvisation: In praise of Charlie, the dandy, who feeds the girls on candy, drinks the apple-brandy, etc.

BLUEBIRD, ii: A rhythmical, rimeless, endless improvisation, in which are woven the "calls" of the dance, beginning:

Yonder goes the bluebird through the window,Down in Tennessee.

THE RAILROAD, ii: To be characterized as the above, yet totally different, beginning:

Out on the railroad, O Jubilee,Waiting for my darling, O Jubilee.

THE BOATMAN, ii: In general form and function like the above, beginning:

Here she sits in her sad station.

LONG SUMMER DAY, ii: In general form and function like the above, beginning:

Skate around the ocean,In a long summer day.

A-MOANING AND GROANING, ii: In general form and function like the above, beginning:

A-moaning and groaning,And that shall be the cry.

MARCHING ROUND THE LEVY [LADY?]: In general form and function like the above, beginning:

We're marching round the levy,For we have gained the day.

GOING TO BOSTON: In general form and function like the above, beginning:

Now we'll promenade, one, two, three,So early in the morning.

HERE COME TWO DUKES A-ROVING, ii: A rhythmical, rimeless improvisation for the men and women of the dance, alternately—beginning:

Here comes two dukes a-roving,With a high-o-ransom-day.

SKIP TO MY LOU, ii: A rhythmical, rimeless chant made up of the dance "calls," beginning:

Steal your partner, skip to my lou,Skip to my lou, my darling.

FOL DOL SOL, 4a3b4c3b, 2ca: One quatrain is:

If you love me as I love you,We have not long to tarry;We'll keep the old folks fixing upFor you and me to marry.

GREEN GROWS THE WILLOW, 4aaaa, 4ca: One quatrain is:

Green grow the rashes O,Green grow the rashes O,Kiss her quick and let her go,For yonder comes her mammy O.

THE JOLLY MILLER, iii, metre as follows, 2:

Jolly is the miller that lives by the mill,The wheel goes round with a right good will,One hand in the hopper and the other in the sack—The boys step forward and the girls step back.

SISTER PHOEBE, 4aab, 2: It begins:

Old sister Phoebe, how happy were weThe night we sat under the juniper tree,The juniper tree, heigh ho, heigh ho.

NEEDLE'S EYE, as follows:

Needle's eye that doth supplyThe thread that runs so true;Many a beau have I let goBecause I wanted you.

GREEN GRAVEL, 4aabb, 4ca: It begins:

Green gravel, green gravel, the grass is so green;You're the prettiest maiden that ever was seen.

[OLD QUEBEC], ii, 4a3b4c3b, 3ca: It begins:

We're marching down to Old Quebec,Where the fifes and drums are beating;America has gained the dayAnd the British are retreating.

[SISTER FRANKIE], 3abcb and 3abcb, 3: The refrain is:

Twice one is twoAnd one and two is three;Dance around the maypoleJust like me.

BUFFALO, ii, 4a3b4c3b, 2: It begins:

Come along, my dearest dear,Present to me your hand;We are roaming in successionTo some far and distant land.

BOUQUET PATCH (PAWPAW PATCH), ii: An endless, rimeless improvisation, beginning:

Where, oh where, is pretty little Mary?Way down yonder in the bouquet patch.

GO IN AND OUT AT THE WINDOW: An endless, rimeless improvisation containing the dance calls in order.

XVIII.

This group contains paralipomena which baffle individual description. It embraces counting-out rimes, jigs, lullabies, child-rimes, nonsense-rimes, and ditties. They are always rhythmical, and usually rimed, varying in length from a couplet to an endless improvisation. The following list is an attempt to name them:

Cluck, Old Hen; Frog in the Meadow; Old as Moses; When I was a Little Boy; Sugar in the Gourd; I'll Build My Nest in a Tree; Old Dan Tucker; Possum up a Gum-stump; By-o Baby Bunting; Peter Punkin-eater; Chickamy Corney-crow; William Trimmel Tram: Shidepoke and Crane; Johnny's out on Picking; Sourwood Mountain; Frisky Jim; Ground-hog; Tarry; Granny, Will Your Dog Bite?; Old Sam Simons; Beefsteak When I'm Hungry; Gray Goose; Needle and Thread; It Rained so Hard; I'll Never get Drunk Anymore; Rock Island; Show Me the Way to Go Home; Sometimes Drunk and Sometimes Sober; Apples in the Summertime; Coony has a Ringy Tail: I Went Down Town; Sally in the Garden; Old Dad; Coon-dog; Rabbit Walked; Shoo, Old Lady, Shine!; Hook and Line; Day I'm Gone; Churn Your Buttermilk; Kalamazine; Hang Down Your Head; I Feel; Shoot Your Dice; Sara Jane; Whickum-whack; Up to the Court-house; Come a High Jim Along; Had an Old Mare; To Rowser's; Roll the Old Chariot Along; Shady Grove; Whangho; Cripple Creek.

www.ingramcontent.com/pod-product-compliance
Ingram Content Group UK Ltd.
Pitfield, Milton Keynes, MK11 3LW, UK
UKHW031846210225
455402UK00004B/325